Freezing and Melting

by Robin Nelson

first step nonfiction

Lerner ... ...polis

Sch

Water can be a **liquid**.

Water in a river is liquid.

Water can be a **solid**.

Water in ice is solid.

Water can change from
a liquid to a solid.

This is called **freezing**.

Water can change from a
solid to a liquid.

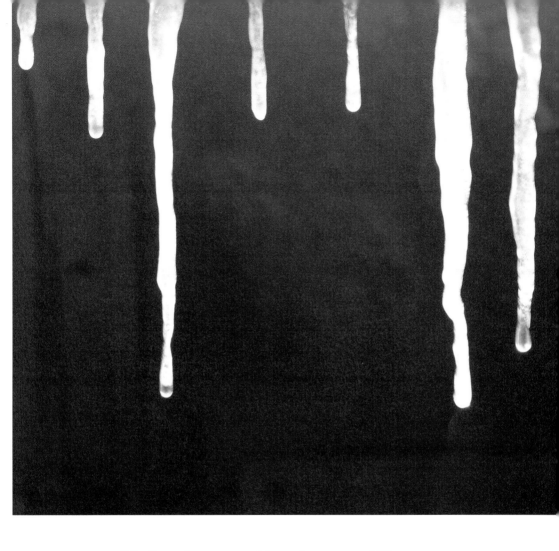

This is called **melting**.

Water freezes when it
gets cold.

Frozen water melts when
it gets warm.

Water freezes into ice cubes.

Ice cubes melt into water.

On a cold day, water
freezes into **icicles**.

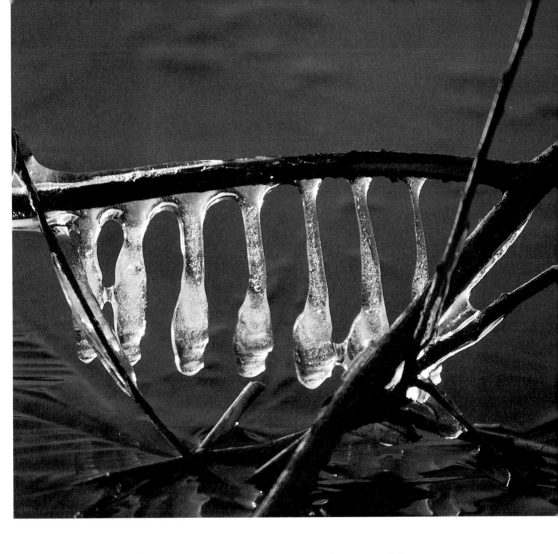

On a warm day, the
icicles melt.

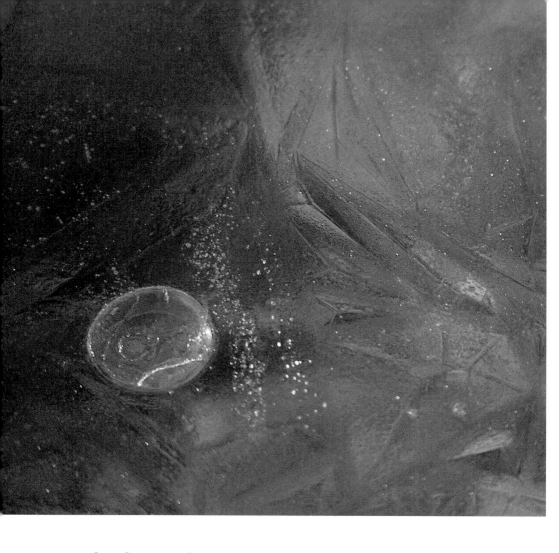

Lakes freeze in the winter.

Snowmen melt in the spring.

Experiment with Water

Water can change from a liquid to a solid and back to a liquid. When water freezes or melts, the amount of water stays the same.

Try this experiment: Measure one cup of water. Freeze it and then let it melt. Measure the amount of water again. It will still be one cup of water.

STEP 1

—1 cup

STEP 2

frozen green
BEANS

—1 cup

STEP 3

—1 cup

STEP 4

—1 cup

19

Freezing and Melting Facts

 Water freezes at 32° F (0° C).

 Water expands when it freezes. If you put a full bottle of water in the freezer, it will explode or break the bottle. The water in the bottle takes up more room when it freezes.

 Glaciers are large masses of ice that move very slowly over land. They are formed from snow on the tops of high mountains.

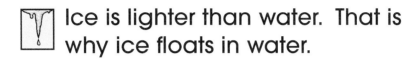 Ice is lighter than water. That is why ice floats in water.

Lakes freeze from the top down. Under the ice on a lake there is still liquid water. This is how fish survive cold winters.

Icebergs are large blocks of glaciers that break off and float away. Icebergs from Antarctica are huge and can be more than 40 miles long.

Glossary

 freezing – changing from a liquid to a solid

 icicles – hanging pieces of ice formed by dripping water

 liquid – something that you can pour

 melting – changing from a solid to a liquid

 solid – something with a shape; not a liquid or a gas

Index

The photographs in this book are reproduced through the courtesy of: © Stephen Graham Photography, front cover, pp. 3, 6, 7, 14, 22 (top, second from top); © Robert Maust/Photo Agora, pp. 2, 22 (middle); National Science Foundation, pp. 4, 10; © Trinity Muller/Independent Picture Service, pp. 5, 22 (bottom); Minneapolis Public Library, p. 8; PhotoDisc, p. 9; © Stuart Klipper, pp. 11, 22 (second from bottom); © Todd Strand/Independent Picture Service, 12, 13; © Greg Vande Leest /Photo Agora, p. 15, 16; © Phillip & Karen Smith/SuperStock, p. 17.

Illustration on page 19 is by Tim Seeley.

Lerner Publications Company
A division of Lerner Publishing Group
241 First Avenue North
Minneapolis, MN 55401 USA

Website address: www.lernerbooks.com

Library of Congress Cataloging-in-Publication Data

Nelson, Robin, 1971–
    Freezing and melting / by Robin Nelson.
        p.   cm. — (First step nonfiction)
    Summary: Summarizes how water changes from a solid to a liquid and back again, and intro-duces related facts such as that water freezes at thirty-two degrees Fahrenheit and that ice floats.
    Includes index.
    ISBN: 0–8225–4590–X (lib. bdg. : alk. paper)
    1. Freezing points—Juvenile literature. 2. Melting points—Juvenile literature. [1. Solids. 2. Liquids. 3. Water.] I. Title. II. Series.
    QD545 .N45 2003
    536'.42—dc21   2002007189

Manufactured in the United States of America
1 2 3 4 5 6 – JR – 08 07 06 05 04 03